PLATO IN 90 MINUTES

Plato
IN 90 MINUTES

Paul Strathern

IVAN R. DEE
CHICAGO

PLATO IN 90 MINUTES. Copyright © 1996 by Paul Strathern.
All rights reserved, including the right to reproduce this book or
portions thereof in any form. For information, address: Ivan R.
Dee, Inc., 1332 North Halsted Street, Chicago 60622.
Manufactured in the United States of America and printed on
acid-free paper.

Library of Congress Cataloging-in-Publication Data:
Strathern, Paul, 1940–
    Plato in 90 minutes / Paul Strathern.
      p.   cm. — (Philosophers in 90 minutes)
    Includes bibliographical references and index.
    ISBN 1-56663-126-2 (cloth : alk. paper). —
    ISBN 1-56663-127-0 (paper : alk. paper)
    1. Plato. I. Title. II. Series.
B395.S768   1996
184—dc20   96-24884

Contents

Introduction 7

Plato's Life and Works 15

Afterword 51

From Plato's Writings 55

Chronology of Significant Philosophical Dates 71

Chronology of Plato's Life 77

Chronology of Plato's Era 79

Recommended Reading 81

Index 83

PLATO IN 90 MINUTES

Introduction

Plato was the ruin of philosophy, or so some modern thinkers would have us believe. According to both Nietzsche and Heidegger, philosophy never recovered from the attentions of Socrates and Plato in the fifth century B.C. Philosophy had been under way less than two hundred years, and in many ways it had scarcely started. But this was where seemingly it went wrong.

Socrates wrote nothing down. Our main knowledge of him is the quasi-historical character who appears in the dialogues of Plato. It is often difficult to know when this character is putting forward the ideas expressed by the actual Socrates, or simply acting as a mouthpiece for Plato's ideas. Either way, this figure differed radically from the philosophers who had preceded him (now generally known as the Pre-Socratics).

So how did Socrates and Plato ruin philosophy before it had properly started? Apparently they made the mistake of treating it as a rational pursuit. The introduction of analysis and cogent argument spoiled the whole thing.

But what was this precious Pre-Socratic tradition that was destroyed by the introduction of reason? The Pre-Socratic philosophers included a number of brilliant oddballs who asked all kinds of profound questions. "What is reality?" "What is existence?" "What is being?" Many of these questions remain unanswered by philosophers to this day (and this includes those modern philosophers who refuse to play the game by claiming that such questions can't be asked in the first place).

By far the most interesting (and most odd) of the Pre-Socratics was Pythagoras. Today Pythagoras is best remembered for his theorem that equates the squares of the sides of a right-angle triangle to the square of its hypotenuse. For centuries this theorem has provided many with their first genuine mathematical understanding—that they will never understand mathematics. It was Pythagoras who most deeply influenced Plato, and to him we must go for the source of many of Plato's ideas.

Pythagoras was more than just a philosopher. He also managed to combine the roles of religious leader, mathematician, mystic, and dietary adviser. This taxing intellectual feat was to leave its mark on his philosophical ideas.

Pythagoras was born on Samos around 580 B.C., but he fled the local tyranny to set up his religious-philosophical-mathematical-dietary school at the Greek colony of Crotone in southern Italy. Here he issued a long list of rules to his pupil-disciple-mystic-gourmets. Among other prohibitions, they were expressly forbidden to eat beans or heart, to break first into a loaf of bread, or to let swallows nest in their roofs—and under no circumstances was one of them to eat his own dog. According to Aristotle, Pythagoras also found time to perform a few miracles, though uncharacteristically Aristotle gives no details of them. In the view of Bertrand Russell, Pythagoras was "a combination of Einstein and Mrs. Eddy" (the founder of Christian Science).

Alas, Pythagoras's impressive range of credentials failed to impress the citizens of Crotone. Eventually they grew tired of all this, and Pythagoras was forced to flee once more. He settled down the road at Metaponto, where he died around 500 B.C. His teachings were to flourish for another hundred years or so, spread throughout southern Italy and Greece by his mystic mathematical disciples. In this way Plato came to hear of Pythagoras.

Like Socrates, Pythagoras took the precaution of writing nothing down. His teachers have peen passed on to us only through the works of his disciples. We now know that Pythagoras's disciples were responsible for much of the motley of thought, practice, mathematics, philosophy, and bats-in-the-belfry that is today labeled Pythagorianism. Indeed, Pythagoras's famous theorem concerning the square of the hypoteneuse was almost certainly not discovered by Pythagoras himself. (Hearteningly for nonmathematicians, this means that Pythagoras too did not understand Pythagoras's Theorem.)

Plato was to be deeply influenced by Pythagoras's famous saying, "All is number." This is the key to Pythagoras's purely philosophical thinking, which was as profound as it was influential. Pythagoras believed that beyond the jumbled world of appearances there lies an abstract harmonious world of number. In fact, his conception of number was closer to what we would call "form." Material objects were not composed of matter but consisted ultimately of the forms—the shapes and structures—out of which they were created. The ideal world of number (or forms) was filled with harmony and was more real than the so-called real world. It was Pythagoras, or the Pythagoreans, who discovered the connection between number and musical harmony. In light of this discovery, Pythagoras's theory of forms (or number) does not seem so far-fetched. Just as it does not seem so far-fetched in the light of modern subatomic physics, which readily resorts to number and descriptions of form rather than definitions of substance.

Such unsubstantial thinking was a frequent characteristic of Pre-Socratic thinking. Pythagoras's disciple Heraclitus, for instance, believed that all is flux. He declared: "No man steps into the same river twice." Yet curiously, this points away from the concern with pure form, presaging the thought of another Pre-Socratic, Democritus. It was he who insisted that the universe is made up of atoms. Democritus arrived at this conclusion well over two thousand years before modern scientists decided that perhaps he was right. Philosophers also took a similar length of time to reach the same conclusion as the Ionian Pre-Socratic Xenophanes, who declared candidly: "No man knows, or ever will know, the truth about the gods and about everything; for even if one happened by chance to say the complete truth, nevertheless one would not know it." This statement is uncannily similar to the views expressed in the twentieth century by Wittgenstein.

Such was the rich and varied philosophical tradition out of which Plato grew.

Plato's Life and Works

Plato was a well-known wrestler, and the name by which we know him today was his ring name. Plato means broad or flat: presumably in this case the former meaning, referring to his shoulders (or, as some sources insist, to his forehead). At his birth in 428 B.C. Plato was given the name Aristocles. He was born in Athens, or on the island of Aegina, which lies just twelve miles offshore from Athens in the Saronic Gulf. Plato was born into one of the great political families of Athens. His father Ariston was descended from Codrus, the last king of Athens, and his mother was descended from the great Athenian lawmaker Solon.

Like any bright member of a political family, Plato's earliest ambitions were in other fields. Twice he carried off the wrestling prize at the Isthmian Games but seemingly never made it to the Olympics at Olympia. Instead he set about trying to become a great tragic poet, but he failed to impress the judges in any of the major competitions. Having failed to win an Olympic gold, or carry off the ancient Greek equivalent of the Nobel Prize, Plato was almost resigned to becoming a mere statesman. Then, as a last fling, he decided to have a go at philosophy, and went off to listen to Socrates.

It was love at first sight. For the next nine years Plato sat at the feet of his master, absorbing all he could of his ideas. Socrates' combative teaching methods forced his pupil to realize his full intellectual potential, at the same time opening his eyes to the unrealized possibilities of the subject.

Socrates taught by a conversational method in which the subject under discussion was gradually analyzed and defined. This method known as *dialectic*—from the ancient Greek word for discussion or disputation (dialect has the same root). Socrates would encourage his conversational protagonist (or pupil) to put forward a definition of some particular topic, and would then proceed to question this—discovering its weaknesses, its strong points, suggesting additions, qualifications, extending the range of the topic, and so forth.

It's difficult for us to imagine the profoundly innovative nature of this method, which relied heavily on reason. Philosophy before Socrates had had little or nothing to do with reason. The Pre-Socratics were for the most part more interested in such topics as Being—the metaphysical nature of what it means to be alive—or the ultimate nature of the world itself (speculating that it might be composed of water, or atoms). A few of these wild-and-woolly intuitions were uncannily accurate, given the way they were arrived at, but it was Socrates who realized that philosophy couldn't go on like this. Philosophers were already a laughingstock, but there was no reason why philosophy itself should be relegated to this category. If philosophical thought was to stop itself from becoming an intellectual joke, or slipping back into religious speculation (from which it had emerged), it needed a more rigorous approach. This was supplied by Socrates' dialectal method. With the benefit of well over two thousand years of hindsight, we can now see this as the forerunner of logic—which was to be invented by Plato's pupil Aristotle a century or so later.

Socrates' achievement, and his pupil Plato's understanding of this, marked a crucial stage in the evolution of philosophy. To appreciate the full extent of this advance, one need only imagine a serious intellectual discussion devoid of reason.

Yet despite having found his true métier, Plato was still tempted to become a backslider and enter politics. Fortunately he was dissuaded by the behavior of Athenian politicians. When the Thirty Tyrants took over after the Peloponnesian War, two of their leaders (Critias and Charmides) were close relatives. The reign of terror that followed might have inspired a young Stalin or Machiavelli, but it didn't impress Plato.

18

After the democrats took over, Plato's beloved teacher was tried on trumped-up charges of impiety and corrupting youth, and sentenced to death. In Plato's eyes, democracy was now tarred with the same brush as tyranny.

Plato's close association with Socrates placed him in a dangerous position, and he was forced to remove himself from Athens for his own good. Thus began his travels, which were to last for the next twelve years. After learning all he could at the feet of his master, he would now learn from the world. But the world wasn't that large in those days, and for the first period of his exile Plato studied just twenty miles away in the neighboring territory of Megara, with his friend Euclid. (This was not the famous geometer but a former pupil of Socrates who had become renowned for the subtlety of his dialectic. Euclid had so loved Socrates that he had traveled through enemy Athenian territory disguised as a woman to be present at the death of his master.)

Plato stayed with Euclid in Megara for three years, then journeyed to Cyrene in North Africa to study with the mathematician Theodorus.

After this he seems to have traveled on to Egypt. According to one persistent story, he now wished to visit some magi in the Levant and ended up traveling east as far as the banks of the Ganges, but this seems unlikely.

Possibly during his stay in Megara, or during a stop on his travels, Plato wrote his earliest extant works. These are in the form of dialogues and are heavily influenced by Socrates, both personally and intellectually. Yet Plato was not completely in his shadow. These dialogues are the creation of a consummate mind—great works of literature as well as philosophy. In many of them Socrates makes an appearance as a leading character and puts forward his ideas. He comes across as infuriating, brilliant, but ultimately endearing, a complex blend of the buffoon and the saint.

No less than three of Plato's early dialogues—*The Apology, Crito*, and *Euthyphron*—as well as the later *Phaedo*, are devoted to the trial, prison days, and ultimate death of Socrates. These events had a profound effect on Plato, and his description of them ranks along-

side *Hamlet* and Dante's *Inferno* in Western literature. *The Apology* describes Socrates' trial
and the seventy-year-old philosopher's defense of
himself before the people of Athens. As a legal or
even a convincing defense, this is flimsy to say
the least. Socrates treated the charge with the
contempt it deserved and moved on to more interesting topics, such as why he was considered
to be wise. He maintained that he was merely
living up to the role proclaimed for him by the
Delphic Oracle, which had described him as the
wisest man on earth. At first he had been suspi-
cious of this pronouncement, as he knew nothing (a typical Socratic claim). So he had begun
questioning others reputed to be wise, and discovered that in truth they knew nothing too.
This is a classic example of the dialectic method:
philosophy being used to reduce contemporary
thinking to ruins. It bears a curious resemblance
to Wittgenstein's linguistic analysis in modern-
day philosophy. Indeed, what Socrates taught
was not so much a philosophy as philosophic
method: clear thinking. This he saw as not only
a means to arriving at the truth but also a way to

good behavior. He would certainly have concurred with Wittgenstein's twentieth-century claim: "Philosophy is not a theory but an activity." Such an attitude leaves an essential vacuum at the heart of philosophic thinking. After Socrates, this was to be filled by Plato.

After more than a decade of traveling, Plato arrived in Sicily, where he visited the crater of Mount Etna. This was a great tourist attraction of the period, and not just as a geographical phenomenon. This, people believed, was what the underworld looked like, and a visit to Etna thus afforded an instructive glimpse of future living conditions. But the crater held an even greater attraction for Plato, owing to its association with Empedocles, the fifth-century philosopher-poet. Empedocles had been gifted with such prodigious intellectual powers that he had eventually become convinced he was a god, and had plunged into the boiling lava of Etna to prove it.

More important, here Plato also made contact with the followers of Pythagoras, who flourished throughout the Greek colonies of Sicily and southern Italy. Pythagoras's discovery of the relation between number and musical harmony had led him to believe that numbers held the key to understanding the universe. Everything could be explained in terms of number, which existed in an abstract realm beyond the everyday world. This theory had a profound effect on Plato, who came to believe that the ultimate reality was abstract. What began as numbers with Pythagoras was to become forms or pure ideas in Plato's philosophy.

The central feature of Plato's philosophy is his Theory of Ideas (or Forms), which he continued to develop all his life. This means that Plato's theory has come down to us in several differing versions, thus providing philosophers with sufficient material to argue over for centuries to come. (No philosophical theory can hope to last the pace unless it has room for argument about how it should be interpreted.)

The best explanation of Plato's Theory of Ideas is his own (which is not always the case, in philosophy as elsewhere). Unfortunately Plato's explanation comes in the form of an image, which places it in the realm of literature rather than philosophy. Briefly, Plato explains that most human beings live as if in a dim cave. We are chained, he says, and facing a blank wall, with a fire at our backs. All we see are flickering shadows playing across the cave wall, and this we take to be reality. Only if we learn to turn away from the wall and the shadows, and escape from the cave, can we hope to see the true light of reality.

In more philosophical terms, Plato believed that everything we perceive around us—the shoes and ships and sealing wax, and cabbages and kings, of everyday experience—is merely appearance. The true reality is the realm of ideas or forms from which this appearance derives. Thus a particular black horse can be said to derive its appearance from the universal form of a horse and from the ideal of blackness. The physical world we perceive with the senses is in a continual state of change. By contrast, the universal realm of ideas, which is perceived by the mind, is unchanging and eternal. Each form—such as that of roundness, man, color, beauty, and so forth—is like a pattern for the particular objects

24

of the world. But the particular objects are only imperfect, ever-changing copies of these universal ideas. With the rational use of the mind we can refine our notions of these universal ideas and begin to apprehend them better. In this way we can approach the ultimate reality of daylight which lies beyond the dim cave of our everyday world.

This realm of universal ideas has a hierarchy, leading from lesser forms to more rarefied abstract ideas, the highest of which is the idea of good. When we learn to ignore the world of ever-changing particulars and concentrate on the timeless reality of ideas, our understanding can begin to rise through the hierarchy of ideas to an ultimate mystical apprehension of the ideas of Beauty, Truth, and ultimately Goodness.

This leads us to Plato's ethics. By concentrating on the particular world, all we can perceive is apparent good. Only with the help of reason can we gain an insight into the greater universal idea of good. Here Plato advocates a morality of spiritual enlightenment rather than any particular rules of conduct. His Theory of

Ideas has also been criticized for its lack of practicality. Taking Plato at his word, it has been suggested that all he describes is simply an idea of the world rather than the world itself. Others claim that Plato's world of ideas exists only in the mind and has little to do with the world from which these ideas are derived. On the other hand, the essentially transcendental nature of Plato's philosophy meant that much of its thinking was later to become acceptable to Christianity.

Plato's theory of creation, for instance, fits easily into the Judeo-Christian version. According to Plato: "The father and creator made a moving living creature in image of the eternal gods. When he saw this creature he was filled with joy and decided to make it even more like its original. Since this original was eternal, he endeavored to make the universe eternal, as far as this could be done. So he made a moving image of eternity. When he laid out the heavens he made this image eternal but moving, in accord with numbers—distinct from eternity which is one and at rest. This moving image is what we call time."

This reads in part like an abstract echo of the Book of Genesis (which was written some eight hundred years before the Pythagorean conception from which it is derived). Yet the explanation of time that Plato gives here—a "moving image of eternity"—is more than a profound religious explanation (and more than a profoundly beautiful explanation). It is profound philosophy. His explanation of time plausibly joins the numerical world of particulars that we live in to the timeless unity of the world of ideas.

Time has always been one of the trickiest notions for philosophers to deal with. It is also one of the least rewarding: we all know time, and it goes on inexorably, regardless of what anyone has to say about it. We all think we know what it is, but it is extremely difficult to describe it in terms that aren't tautologous (e.g., "Time is succession") or vacuous (e.g., "Time is but the stream I go a-fishing in."—Thoreau).

Plato's explanation was a superb poetic-philosophic image which not only fitted precisely into his Theory of Ideas but also appeared to be the linchpin that held it together. (It has been called "the perfect-fitting cog, whose movement drives each part of everything as one"—but this fine mechanistic image is inexact, as the world of abstract ideas does not move and is not driven by time.)

Since Plato, few have offered as convincing an explanation of time. It was another seven centuries before St. Augustine produced a theory of similar caliber. For him, time was merely our subjective way of viewing the universe. This is essentially Plato's theory turned outside in. During the fifteen hundred years since St. Augustine, only Kant's explanation of time is its peer. And this too is subjective (when it would seem obvious that time is no such thing). Essentially Kant believed that time is part of our perceptual apparatus (like irremovable spectacles) through which we see the world. But it remains Plato's explanation that best matches the latest scientific theories of time. "When he laid out the heavens he made this image eternal but moving, in accord with numbers." In other words, time and the universe started at the same instant. This concurs with the Big Bang theory, which states that we can't speak of "before" the Big Bang because time didn't exist then.

Science and philosophy are essentially different ways of looking at the world: they are categorically separate. As Bernard de Mandeville put it, "One deals with what is, the other wonders why." Even so, it's always reassuring when science and philosophy are in agreement. And when the philosophy in question dates from the scientific era where the most powerful form of locomotive energy was galley slaves, one can only marvel.

While Plato was in Sicily he became a close friend of Dion, brother-in-law of Dionysius, the ruler of Syracuse. Dion took his new friend to meet Dionysius, possibly with the hope of procuring for him an appointment as philosopher-in-residence at the court. But despite Plato's travels through the world he remained very much an aristocratic Athenian and was not taken with the provincial ways of the Syracusan court. Dionysius was an army officer and a tyrant who also had inflated literary pretensions and believed himself to be twice the man of any of his contemporaries. He married two women, Doris and Aristomache, on the same day, and on his wedding night had them both in his bed.

Things seem to have quieted a bit by the time Plato arrived on the scene. It all sounds rather pleasant from his description, even if he "found nothing to please me in the tastes of a society devoted to Italian cuisine, where happiness was held to consist in stuffing oneself twice a day and never sleeping alone at night." This was evidently too much stuffing for the forty-year-old Plato, whose Athenian fastidiousness soon got on Dionysius's nerves.

Dionysius had begun life as a clerk in the civil administration but had been marked out from the start by his exceptional poetic gifts. He had then risen through the ranks of the army, at the same time composing a few verse tragedies of unsurpassed merit (as all his subordinate officers readily agreed). After seizing power he transformed Syracuse, by a series of brutal conquests, into the most powerful Greek city west of Greece. In order to smooth diplomatic relations, the Athenians made sure that his drama *The Ransom of Hector* was awarded a prize at the Lenaen Festival.

Dionysius was not the kind of man to let himself be cowed by some philosophic nob who was trying to cadge a job at his court. When he and Plato turned to discussing philosophy, the sparks soon began to fly. At one point Plato found himself forced to point out a flaw in Dionysius's thinking.

"You speak like a geriatric fool," exclaimed Dionysius in disgust.

"And you speak like a tyrant," replied Plato.

Whereupon Dionysius decided to live up to the philosopher's observation and had Plato clapped in irons. Plato was placed on a Spartan ship bound for Aegina, where the captain was instructed to sell Plato as a slave. "Don't worry, he's so much of a philosopher he won't even notice," remarked Dionysius.

Some sources have maintained that Plato's life was in danger at this point. But the fact that he was sent to Aegina suggests otherwise and indicates that this island was probably his place of birth, rather than Athens. Sending Plato back to his birthplace as a slave was just the kind of humiliation that would have appealed to Dionysius. He could also have been fairly certain that Plato would be recognized and bought by some influential friend, thus avoiding serious diplomatic repercussions with Athens.

Dionysius's scheme played out just as he'd planned. Plato was given a nasty fright (the prospect of having to work for a living was enough to strike a chill in the heart of any true philosopher). And it wasn't long before Plato was spotted in the slave market at Aegina by his well-heeled old friend Anniceris the Cyrenaic, who bought him for the bargain price of twenty mina. Anniceris was so pleased with his cut-price philosopher that he sent him back to Athens with enough money to set up a school.

In 386 B.C. Plato bought a plot of land in the Grove of Academe. This was a mile or so northwest of Athens, beyond the Eriai Gate in the ancient city walls. It was a region of parkland dotted with plane trees, in whose shade stood a number of statues and temples. Here, amidst the cool avenues and tinkling streams, Plato opened the Academy, gathering around him a group of followers which unusually included several women, among them Axiothea, who dressed as a man. This is recognizable as the first university.

The Grove of Academe where Plato founded the Academy (and from which the school took its name) was called after a former resident named Hecademus, an obscure semidivine hero of Attic mythology. Hecademus's main accomplishment appears to have been the planting here of twelve olive trees, offshoots from the sacred olive tree of Athena on the Acropolis. Yet as a result of Plato choosing this site, Hecademus is remembered to this day throughout the civilized world, our version of his name adorning everything from secretarial colleges to cinemas, a Scottish football team, and annual awards for similar semidivine figures of obscure accomplishment.

Today the Grove of Academe is a long, straggly stretch of wasteland in northwestern

Athens, where the inner suburbs start to grow ragged at the edges. Beneath the trees next to the bus depot lie scattered ancient stones, occasional piles of dumped domestic refuse, and a few benches covered with graffiti. The site of Plato's Academy, and the house where he lived, are almost certainly lost forever. Astonishingly, Hecademus's home is still there. Beneath the archaeologists' protective tin roof you can see its exposed baked mud foundations and the remains of its mud brick walls, which were already almost two thousand years old by the time Plato set up here. Hecademus seems to have had a knack for immortality.

Meanwhile, just across the wasteland is a modern encampment where conditions comparable to those in Hecademus's prehistoric home still prevail more than four thousand years later. Amidst the cardboard-box dwellings and pools of stagnant water, shaven-headed immigrant children play in the hot sunlight beneath halos of flies while their head-scarfed mothers sit bow-legged among the refuse, suckling naked dark-skinned infants.

"What is Justice?" asks Plato in his best-known work, *The Republic*. In this dialogue he assembles Socrates and a cast of characters for dinner at a retired tycoon's mansion. By the time Socrates takes over the conversation, the company has agreed that there is no point in trying to define justice, except in the larger context of society. So Socrates sets about describing his idea of a just society.

The earlier dialogues written by Plato, but starring Socrates, are generally thought to contain Socrates' ideas. In the middle and later dialogues these ideas undergo something of a transformation, and here the ideas put forward by Socrates are perceived to be Plato's own. *The Republic* is the finest of the middle-period dialogues, and in the course of his prescription for a just society Plato sets out his ideas on such wide-ranging topics as free speech, feminism, birth control, public and private morality, parenthood, psychology, education, public and private ownership, and much more. Just the sort of subjects you might go out of your way to avoid at any enjoyable dinner party. But *The Republic* was not to be an enjoyable dinner party, we soon discover. And the society it proposed was not to be very enjoyable either. Plato's opinions on the topics mentioned above are almost all seriously at odds with the opinions held nowadays by all but earnest bigots and the slightly crazy.

In Plato's ideal republic there would be no possessions or marriage (except among the lower orders, who were presumably the only people fit for such things). Children would be removed from their mothers soon after birth and educated communally. In this way they would come to regard the state as their parents, and all their contemporaries would become brothers and sisters. Until the age of twenty they would be educated in gymnastics and uplifting music. (No Ionian or Lydian music was permitted, only military marches to instill courage and the love of the fatherland.)

All this makes one wonder about Plato's own childhood. Sure enough, we learn from Diogenes Laertius that Plato's father "made violent love" to his mother but "failed to win her." Although Plato was almost certainly born in wedlock, his mother appears to have soon taken a second husband, and Plato was almost certainly brought up in a number of households. So perhaps it's no surprise that Plato had little time for family life.

In Utopia according to Plato, at the age of twenty those who had shown insufficient appreciation of their physical and musical education were weeded out. These were dispatched to do menial tasks such as support the entire community by being farmers and businessmen. Meanwhile the superior students went on to study arithmetic, geometry, and astronomy for ten years. Maddened by mathematics, the next batch of failures was sent to the military. Now only the elite remained. For five years, until they were thirty-five, they were permitted the great honor of studying philosophy; then, for fifteen years, they became involved in the practical study of government, immersing themselves in the ways of the world. At the age of fifty they were considered fit to rule.

These philosopher-rulers lived together in a communal barracks where they had no private possessions and could sleep together as they chose. There was complete equality of men and women (though in another dialogue Plato does let slip that "if the soul fails to live well for its appointed time in a man, it passes into the body of a woman"). Living communally and having no personal interests, this elite would thus be above bribery; and their only ambition would be to ensure justice in the state. From this lot was chosen the head of state, the philosopher-king.

Even for the small ideal city-state ("nine miles from the sea") where this was all intended to take place, it would appear to be a recipe for disaster. At best it would be stupefyingly boring, for all poets, dramatists, and people who played the wrong type of music were banned, as were lawyers. At worst it would be a totalitarian nightmare which would quickly develop all the usual unpleasant methods required to maintain such an unpopular regime.

With hindsight it is easy enough to pick holes in this earnest fantasy. Even Plato's own description involves him in a number of contradictions. Poets were banned, yet Plato himself uses many superb poetic images in the course of his arguments. Likewise worship of the gods, religion, and mythology were forbidden, yet Plato himself includes several myths in this work, and the "philosopher-rulers" bear an uncanny resemblance to a priestly caste. He also introduces an ideal god of his own, who is implacable and must be obeyed (even though his existence cannot be proved).

In fact, Plato's vision of the ideal republic would seem to be strictly a product of its age. Athens had just been defeated by Sparta in the Peloponnesian War. Neither democracy nor tyranny had worked, and Athens desperately needed government that could provide order. (Indeed, some commentators consider that when Plato speaks of justice, what he often means is something more akin to order.) The answer appeared to lie in a strictly controlled society such as that which prevailed in Sparta. But unlike Athens, Sparta was a philistine, economically backward society, which in order to survive had to produce a caste of mindless hooligans willing to obey orders and fight to the death. The task of this caste was to inflict terror on the city's increasingly rebellious lower orders and to cow its sophisticated and economically powerful neighbors. Plato was either ignorant of this or unwilling to take it into account.

In an extension of Socrates' naive ethical belief ("the good are happy"), Plato believed that "the unjust alone are unhappy." Impose a just society, and everyone will be fine. But what did he suggest? Just the kind of blueprint you'd expect from an earnest, high-minded intellectual closeted in the Grove of Academe. It could never work.

Yet the astonishing thing is that it *did*. Or something like it did. For over a millennium medieval society, with its lower orders, its military caste, and its powerful priesthood, bore a remarkable resemblance to Plato's republic. In more recent times, communism and fascism have adopted many of the republic's essential features.

For several years Plato continued to teach at his Academy, establishing it as the finest school in Athens. Then in 367 B.C. he heard from his friend Dion that Dionysius, the tyrant of Syracuse, had died, and that his son Dionysius (the Younger) had succeeded him.

For years Dionysius the Younger had been kept locked up by his father in order to thwart any ambitions he might have harbored about premature succession. Incarcerated in the royal palace, Dionysius the Younger had spent his days industriously sawing up pieces of wood, constructing tables and stools.

According to Dion, this was the perfect opportunity for Plato. Here was the ideal ruler for him to instruct in the ways of the philosopher-king. His mind would be uncluttered by other ideas, and Plato could put his theoretical republic into practice.

For some reason Plato didn't find this prospect appealing. (Perhaps he was worried about the position of a sixty-one-year-old who arrived to take up residence in the ideal republic. Would he too have to undergo a prolonged regime of gymnastics and military music before he could join the elite?) But in the end "my fear of losing my self-respect, and becoming in my own eyes a creature of mere words who never put them into practice," forced Plato to succumb to the entreaties of his friend, and he set out on the long journey to Sicily.

When Plato arrived he found the court of Dionysius the Younger seething with intrigue. A number of influential courtiers remembered the intellectual dandy from his previous visit, and some of them appeared to have it in for Dion as well. Within a few months these enemies of philosophy contrived to have both Plato and Dion accused of treason. (A frequent pitfall for those who scheme to set up a utopia.) At first the carpenter-king wasn't sure what to do. Then, fearful of Dion's power, he banished his uncle but refused to allow Plato to leave. He didn't want Plato saying bad things about him when he returned to Athens, he informed the old philosopher.

Fortunately friends soon managed to engineer Plato's escape, and he returned to Athens where his faithful disciples and Dion were waiting for him at the Academy.

But Dionysius the Younger was hurt by Plato's defection. He had greatly enjoyed his conversations about philosophy with Plato, even if he had no intention of putting any of his ideas into practice. (Syracuse was hardly in a position to indulge in such experiments. At the time it was the one strong state managing to resist the encroachment of Carthage into Italy, where it would have overrun the embryo Roman republic.)

Dionysius the Younger seems to have begun to look upon Plato as a kind of father figure. He was certainly jealous of Plato's affection for his uncle Dion. Dionysius the Younger continued to pester Plato with requests for his return to Syracuse. Distraught, Dionysius declared to all who would listen to him that his life was no longer worth living without the company of his philosophy instructor. In the end he sent his fastest trireme to Athens and threatened to confiscate all of Dion's possessions in Syracuse (which were considerable) if Plato did not come to see him.

Eventually, against his better judgment, the seventy-one-year-old Plato set sail for Syracuse. He appears to have been persuaded by Dion, who at this stage might well have been influenced by other concerns than the possibility of setting up Plato's utopia and "the idea of demonstrating to the tyrant the primacy of the soul over the body."

Within no time Plato was once again a virtual prisoner in Syracuse, doubtless twice a day refusing to stuff himself with Italian cuisine, and angrily evicting undesirables from his bed each night. But fortunately Plato was once again rescued, this time with the help of a sympathetic Pythagorean from Taranto, who came to fetch him at dead of night in his trireme. With the galley slaves heaving valiantly beneath the lash, the aged philosopher sped back across the sea toward the safety of Athens. (Some years later Dion was to succeed in what had perhaps been his aim all along: he invaded Syracuse, ousted Dionysius the Younger, and took power himself. Did he attempt to set up Plato's Republic, now that he at last had the chance? Apparently not. But poetic justice was to succeed where platonic justice did not. Dion was shortly assassinated—betrayed, curiously enough, by a former disciple of Plato's.)

Thus ended Plato's sorties into the political sphere—the Roman Empire was safe. Yet as a result of his untried theories, the medieval world that was to grow out of the Roman Empire would have a model; and later the likes of Stalin and Hitler would have a classical precedent for their endeavors.

Was Plato entirely wrongheaded? In his view true knowledge or understanding can only be apprehended by the intellect, not by the senses. The mind must withdraw from the world of experience if it is to reach the truth. If Plato seriously believed this, it's very difficult to understand what on earth he was doing legislating for his utopia in the first place. Such a philosophic view is incompatible with the practice of politics. Yet according to Plato, "Unless philosophers become rulers, or rulers study philosophy, there will be no end to the troubles of men." (In practice, it's turned out precisely the opposite. Rulers inspired by philosophical ideas have caused far more trouble than philosophical ignoramuses.)

The nonpolitical part of Plato's philosophy was also to prove a major influence for many centuries to come. This was largely because it blended well with Christianity, lending what had begun as mere faith a more sound philosophical foundation. (As a result, it wasn't just enough to disbelieve in Christianity, you had to disprove it too.)

For Plato the human soul consisted of three distinct elements. The rational element strove for wisdom, the active spirit sought conquest and distinction, and the appetites craved gratification. (These elements are echoed in the three elements of society which Plato describes in *The Republic*: the philosophers, the men of action or soldiers, and the dross who merely kept the whole thing going and believed in enjoying themselves.) The righteous man is governed by reason, but all three elements have their part to play. We could not continue without satisfying our appetites, just as the entire state would grind to a halt if the workers gave up working and enjoying themselves, and instead tried to become philosophers. The point is that righteousness can be achieved only when each of the three elements of the soul is fulfilling its own function—much as justice is achieved in the state only when each of the three social elements is fulfilling its role in society.

By far the most enjoyable of Plato's dialogues is *The Symposium*, which is devoted to a discussion of love in its various manifestations. The ancient Greeks were not prudish about erotic love, and the section where Alcibiades describes his homosexual love for Socrates ensured that this book would later be widely suppressed—becoming the original underground classic in the cellars of medieval monasteries. (New editions of *The Symposium* were solemnly placed on the Index of Banned Books by the Catholic church until 1966.)

In Plato, eros is regarded as the soul's impulse toward good. In its lowest form this is expressed in our passion for a beautiful person and our wish for immortality by producing offspring with that person (although it is difficult to see how this applied to Alcibiades, for Socrates was no beauty, and there was no possibility of any offspring here). A higher form of love involves a union devoted to more spiritual aspirations, giving rise to social good. The highest form of platonic love is devoted to philosophy, and the pinnacle of this is the achievement of a mystic vision of the idea of the good.

Plato's ideas on love were to have a profound influence. They crop up in the notion of courtly love, so popular with the troubador poets of the early Middle Ages. Some even see in Plato's understanding of eros an early blueprint for the more lurid sexual fantasies of Freud. Today the notion of platonic love has been debased to the point where it describes an almost extinct form of attraction between the sexes. Even Plato's Theory of Ideas, intended to lead us to the mystical apprehension of Beauty, Truth, and Goodness, has now been stripped of much of its ethereal grandeur. Critics point out that this theory merely supposes that the world works like language, with abstract words and concepts assuming the higher ground. This may be a mistaken assumption, but we have not yet fully rid ourselves of it. Plato suggested that the actual world isn't the same as we apprehend and describe it through experience and language.

And why should it be? Indeed, it seems unlikely that it is. But how can we ever tell?

At the age of eighty-one Plato died and was buried in the Academy. Despite the unlikelihood of his philosophy, many of its assumptions still linger in our attitude toward the world. And the adjective derived from his name continues to describe an increasingly unlikely form of love, which touchingly echoes his Theory of Ideas. Plato's Academy was to flourish in Athens until it was finally closed by the Emperor Justinian in 529 A.D., in his attempt to suppress pagan Hellenistic culture in favor of Christianity. This date is now regarded by many historians as marking the end of Greco-Roman culture and the start of the Dark Ages.

Afterword

Just as Socrates was followed by his pupil Plato, so Plato was followed by his pupil Aristotle—thus completing the triumvirate of great Greek philosophers. Aristotle developed and criticized Plato's thought, introducing many of his own ideas, and in the process created a philosophy of his own. But Plato's philosophy in its purer form continued to flourish at the Academy, where it became known as Platonism.

With the advent of the Roman Empire, this philosophy gradually spread, shedding various aspects of Plato's philosophy along the way. Quite obviously, any discussion of political utopias was unwise in an empire run by the likes of Caligula or Nero. Other ideas, such as those on mathematics, were simply ignored because the Romans weren't interested in mathematics.

Over the years Platonism began to evolve. A number of its most loyal practitioners eventually concluded that although Plato's philosophy was correct, Plato himself often hadn't known what he was talking about. These philosophers decided that *they* knew what Plato was talking about, and the result was a new version of Plato's philosophy known as Neoplatonism. In general the Neoplatonists emphasized the mystical elements of Platonism. They tended to believe in a hierarchy of being which ascends from multiplicity to the utter simplicity of the Good (or the One).

The chief exponent of Neoplatonism was the third-century philosopher Plotinus, who was educated in Alexandria. Plotinus was the pupil of a lapsed Christian who had become a Platonist, and some of Plotinus's ideas had an almost Christian tenor. But as Christianity and Neoplatonism spread through the Roman Empire they inevitably came into conflict. For a while Neoplatonism was seen as the main bulwark against the tide of Christianity.

But the fourth century saw the birth of St. Augustine of Hippo, the finest philosophical mind since Aristotle. St. Augustine was troubled by the lack of intellectual content in Christianity and found himself attracted to Neoplatonism. St. Augustine eventually succeeded in reconciling the philosophy of Plotinus with orthodox Christian theology. In this way Christianity was given a firmer intellectual foundation, and the evolved ideas of Plato were grafted onto the only intellectual force that proved able to survive the Dark Ages.

Platonism (of one sort or another) thus became part of the Christian tradition, which through the centuries produced a succession of thinkers who understood Plato better than Plato—the Platonists, the Neoplatonists, St. Augustine, and so forth. Platonists continued to flourish in major European universities—espe-

cially in Germany and at Cambridge—until well
into the twentieth century, but the species is now
thought to be extinct.

From Plato's Writings

Philosophy begins in wonder.
—*Theaetetus*, 155d

Here is a parable which shows how our nature may become enlightened or remain unenlightened. Imagine the condition of men as living in a sort of underground cavern, with a long entrance open to the light. Here men have existed since childhood, fettered by the leg and the neck, so that they cannot move or turn their heads in any way, and can only see in front of them. Higher up, and some distance behind them, is the light of a burning fire; and between the fire and the prisoners is a path with a parapet along it, like the screen at a puppet show which conceals the performers while they display their puppets above it.

I can picture it, he replied.

Now behind the parapet imagine there are men carrying all kinds of objects—including figures of men and animals, in stone and wood and various other materials—which project above the parapet. Some of these people would be speaking, and some would be silent.

This is a strange image you conjure up, he said, and those chained men are strange prisoners.

No, they are just like us, I replied. For, to begin with, do you think such prisoners would see anything of themselves, or of one another, except for the shadows cast by the firelight onto the wall of the cave facing them?

How could they see more if their heads are prevented from turning?

And they would see just as little of the objects being carried past.

Of course.

Now, if they were able to talk to one another, surely they would suppose that in naming the shadows they saw they were in fact naming the actual objects?

Certainly.

And if their prison had an echo from the wall facing them, when one of the passersby behind them spoke the prisoners would naturally assume this came from the shadow passing before their eyes.

By Zeus, they would indeed, he said.

In all ways, then, the prisoners would consider reality to be nothing else than the shadows of those artificial objects.

Inevitably, he agreed.

—*The Republic*, Book VII, 514a–c

We must then conclude that education is not, as some claim, the introducing into a soul of knowledge which was not there beforehand—as if they were introducing sight into a blind eye.

That is what they say it is.

But our argument shows that the capacity

for understanding truth is innate in each man's soul, and that the way in which he learns is like an eye which cannot be turned from the darkness toward the light except by turning the whole body. In the same way the entire soul must be turned away from this world of change and shadows until its eye is able to endure the bright shining light of reality, and the brightest of all realities, which we have called the Good.

—*The Republic*, Book VII, 518b–c

God is blameless.

—*The Republic*, Book X, 617e

Do not forget that popular favor is a way to achievement, whereas an arbitrary temper has solitude for company.

—*Letters*, IV, 321c

A man is just in the same way that a state is just. And we must not forget that justice in the state means that each of the three classes found within it is performing its proper function . . . each of us is just and does his duty only when each part of us performs its proper function. . . .

—*The Republic*, Book IV, 441d (c in some translations)

It is the business of reason to rule, exercising wisdom and foresight on behalf of the entire soul, while the spirited element should act as its subordinate and ally. . . .

When these two elements have been reared and trained to understand their own true functions, they should be set to rule over the mass of our appetites, which make up by far the largest part of our soul, and are by nature insatiable. These ever-demanding appetites must be watched over with constant vigilance, so as to prevent them from gorging themselves on the so-called pleasures of the body, and thus becoming so huge and insatiable that the body no longer fulfils its proper role but instead attempts to overturn and enslave the entire life of man.

—*The Republic*, Book IV, 441e, 442a

I had a dream, and in this dream I was told that the first elements out of which all things including you and I are made, are such that no one can give an explanation of them. Each of them by itself can only be named; we cannot attribute anything further to them. We cannot even say that they exist, or that they do not exist, if we mean to speak of them alone, for to do so would be to imply the attributes of existence or nonexistence. . . .

We cannot define any of these primeval elements. They can only be named, for they have nothing but a name. Yet the things composed of these elements, because they are thus complex, are defined by a combination of names which makes up a description, for a description is the essence of their definition.

—*Theaetetus*, 201e (b in some translations), 202b

Suppose that when someone sees or hears or notices something he says to himself: "What I perceive looks rather like something else, though it is in fact only a poor imitation." Don't you agree that the person who receives this impression must have had previous knowledge of that "something else," and is in fact being reminded of it?

Of course. . . .

Then we must have had some earlier knowledge of equality before we first saw things which were almost equal, without being fully so.

I agree.

And at the same time we agree that we did not and could not have come by this notion of equality except by sight or touch or one of the senses. I am treating them as all being the same.

They are, Socrates, for the purposes of our argument.

So it must be by the senses that we become aware of the notion that things which are almost equal are not absolutely equal. Yet we must have a notion of this absolute equality, or there would be no standard with which to compare the things that we perceive as being almost equal.

That sounds logical enough, Socrates.

But surely we first see and hear and use our senses only at birth?

Of course.

But previously we agreed that we must have knowledge of equivalence and nonequivalence before we use our senses, or we would not be able to make any sense of them.

Yes.

Which means we must have had this knowledge before we were born.

So it appears.

Therefore, if we had this knowledge before we were born, and knew it when we were born, this means we had knowledge not only of equality and relative equivalence, but also of all absolute standards. And this same argument which we applied to absolute equality, applies just as much to the absolutes of beauty, goodness, morality, and holiness. And also, I maintain, to all those characteristics to which we apply the term "absolute." This shows that we must obtain knowledge of such absolutes before we were born.

—*Phaedo*, 73c, 74e (end) *et seq*

It is said that Socrates had a dream about a cygnet which sat on his knees. It quickly grew plumage and became a swan, then flew off, letting out a loud sweet cry. Next day Plato was introduced to Socrates as a pupil, and Socrates immediately recognized him as the swan in his dream.

—Diogenes Laertius, *Lives of the Eminent Philosophers*, Book 3, 5

The other side of Plato:

The strongest principle is that everybody, whether they are male or female, should have a leader. Likewise, no one should get into the habit of doing anything at all on his own initiative—either in earnest or in jest. Both in war and during time of peace, he should respect his leader and follow him faithfully. He should look up to his leader and follow his guidance in even the smallest matters. For example, he should get up, move around, wash, and have his meals . . . only at such times as he has been ordered to do so. In other words, he should get into the habit, by a long process of training, of never even dreaming of acting independently, and thus becoming utterly incapable of such action. In this way the life of all is spent in total community. There is no law, and there never will be one, which is above this. It is the most effective way of achieving salvation and victory in war. And in peacetime, and from earliest childhood, this should remain the highest law—the need to rule others and be ruled by others. All trace of independence or anarchistic spirit must be completely eradicated from the life of all men, and even the wild beasts which are kept by these men.

—*The Laws*, 942a–f

This will all appear chillingly familiar to students of the Third Reich and Communist regimes from Stalinist Russia to the Cultural Revolution. The "political science" of dictatorship appears to have developed little over the past two millennia since the nursery era of our civilization. Just as the psychology that instigates such states evolves little beyond the nursery stage of its development.

For centuries Plato could do no wrong. While he remained the preserve of the classicists and theologians, such views were considered harmless—except by those who became head-masters of elite boarding schools, who used them as a blueprint for Victorian education. Not until the middle of the twentieth century did the Austrian philosopher Karl Popper decided it was time Plato was exposed as a fascist. He did this in The Open Society and Its Enemies, *from which the following argument is taken:*

Individualism, united with altruism, has become the basis of our Western civilization. It is the central doctrine of Christianity ("love thy neighbor," say the Scriptures, not "love your tribe"); and it is the core of all ethical doctrines which have grown from our civilization and stimulated it. . . . Plato was right when he saw in this doctrine the enemy of his caste state; and he hated it more than any other of the "subversive" doc-

trines of his time. . . . Never was a man more in earnest in his hostility toward the individual.
—Popper, *The Open Society and Its Enemies*

Popper quotes the following passage, where Plato describes his Republic as "the highest form of state." Plato continues:

Women and children, as well as all servants, slaves, and livestock, are considered as common property of the state. Every possible means has been taken to obliterate from our life any possible hint of individualism or anything looked upon as private. In as far as it is possible, even the things which nature herself has made private and individual have been transformed into the common property of all. Nothing remains personal: even our eyes, ears, and hands seem to see, hear, and act as if they did not belong to individuals but to the collective community. All are cast in the same mold, so that they are identical to each other to the ultimate degree. They give praise or cast blame with unanimous accord; they even rejoice or sorrow over the same things, all together and at the same times. All the laws are perfected with the aim of unifying the citizens to the ultimate degree possible. . . . It is not possible to discover any better criteria for a more excellent form of state.

—*The Laws*, 739c *et seq*

These are not the extremist views of youth but the considered judgment of wise old age. The Laws *is one of Plato's last works. He almost certainly wrote it after he returned from Syracuse for the third and last time. This would put him in his mid- to late seventies.*

Many commentators seem to concur with the view that in The Laws *"Plato made concessions to real life, modifying the Utopianism of the* Republic*" (Copleston). Leaving aside the question of whether Plato's Republic is a utopia (of any sort, for anyone involved), are these the sort of concessions to real life which we wish to see? A totalitarian state with mass conformism has often, alas, been real life for millions of unfortunates (and continues to be so). But for most* of us the concessions to real life we would wish to see in Plato's Republic are of a somewhat different order.

"All right, since you're not capable of living up to my utopia, I'll give you hell on earth instead," seems to be the gist of Plato's attitude. As I have already suggested, there are strong psychological and historical reasons why Plato believed in such grotesque ideas. But what is the use of philosophy when one of its supreme practitioners advances dangerously wrongheaded notions like this? It is possible to argue that Plato's philosophy (like his world of ideas) transcended his age, whereas his political ideas (like the particulars of the world which we inhabit) were nothing more than a phantasmagoria of spectral half-truths. Indeed, there's no denying that Plato's political ideas were of their time. Athens was under threat and needed to become another Sparta if it were to survive. (Within a decade of Plato's death it was overrun by the Macedonians.) Unfortunately Plato advocates his paranoid regime during both war and peace, during times of threat as well as times when there is no threat, in bad times and not so bad times. (There could be no such thing as good times under such a regime.)

Offensive political ideas are not limited to small cities in the Balkans over two thousand years ago. They continue to flourish. In other words, Plato's political ideas are as timeless as his other philosophy. There appears to be no answer to this. Plato's philosophy was, and remains, one of the great ornaments of Western civilization. It formulated the questions that philosophy still tries to answer, and provided the intellectual foundation for Christian thinking. And yet its social theories are offensive in the extreme. (It's no excuse to say that everyone thought like that in those days. They didn't: Plato lived in Athens, the home of democracy.) Perhaps all we can usefully say is that Plato's grades should read Alpha-plus for philosophy, Gamma-minus for politics.

Chronology of Significant
Philosophical Dates

6th C B.C.   The beginning of Western philosophy
                  with Thales of Miletus.

End of
6th C B.C.   Death of Pythagoras.

399 B.C.   Socrates sentenced to death in
                  Athens.

c 387 B.C.   Plato founds the Academy in Athens,
                  the first university.

335 B.C.   Aristotle founds the Lyceum in
                  Athens, a rival school to the
                  Academy.

324 A.D.	Emperor Constantine moves capital of Roman Empire to Byzantium.
400 A.D.	St. Augustine writes his *Confessions*. Philosophy absorbed into Christian theology.
410 A.D.	Sack of Rome by Visigoths heralds opening of Dark Ages.
529 A.D.	Closure of Academy in Athens by Emperor Justinian marks end of Hellenic thought.
Mid-13th C	Thomas Aquinas writes his commentaries on Aristotle. Era of Scholasticism.
1453	Fall of Byzantium to Turks, end of Byzantine Empire.
1492	Columbus reaches America. Renaissance in Florence and revival of interest in Greek learning.
1543	Copernicus publishes *On the Revolution of the Celestial Orbs*, proving mathematically that the earth revolves around the sun.

1633	Galileo forced by church to recant heliocentric theory of the universe.
1641	Descartes publishes his *Meditations*, the start of modern philosophy.
1677	Death of Spinoza allows publication of his *Ethics*.
1687	Newton publishes *Principia*, introducing concept of gravity.
1689	Locke publishes *Essay Concerning Human Understanding*. Start of empiricism.
1710	Berkeley publishes *Principles of Human Knowledge*, advancing empiricism to new extremes.
1716	Death of Leibniz.
1739–1740	Hume publishes *Treatise of Human Nature*, taking empiricism to its logical limits.
1781	Kant, awakened from his "dogmatic slumbers" by Hume, publishes *Critique of Pure Reason*.

Great era of German metaphysics begins.

1807   Hegel publishes *The Phenomenology of Mind*, high point of German metaphysics.

1818   Schopenhauer publishes *The World as Will and Representation*, introducing Indian philosophy into German metaphysics.

1889   Nietzsche, having declared "God is dead," succumbs to madness in Turin.

1921   Wittgenstein publishes *Tractatus Logico-Philosophicus*, claiming the "final solution" to the problems of philosophy.

1920s   Vienna Circle propounds Logical Positivism.

1927   Heidegger publishes *Being and Time*, heralding split between analytical and Continental philosophy.

1943   Sartre publishes *Being and Nothingness*, advancing

Heidegger's thought and instigating existentialism.

1953   Posthumous publication of Wittgenstein's *Philosophical Investigations*. High era of linguistic analysis.

Chronology of Plato's Life

c 428 B.C.	Birth of Plato on island of Aegina (or in Athens).
399 B.C.	Flees Athens after death of Socrates, travels in North Africa, Middle East, and Italy.
c 388 B.C.	At court of Dionysius I, ruler of Syracuse in Sicily.
c 387 B.C.	Founds the Academy in Athens.
367 B.C.	Returns to Syracuse to instruct Dionysius II, but soon flees.
361–360 B.C.	Returns yet again to the court at Syracuse.
c 347 B.C.	Death of Plato at age eighty-one.

529 A.D.   Closing of Academy by Emperor
Justinian and the start of the
Dark Ages.

Chronology of Plato's Era

438 B.C.	Parthenon built in Athens.
431 B.C.	Free adult male population of Athens calculated at 42,000 (the slave population was probably double this).
430 B.C.	Death of Phidias, sculptor and architect of the Parthenon.
429 B.C.	Death of Pericles, ruler of Athens through its golden era.
415–413 B.C.	Athenian expedition to capture Sicily, ending in disaster.
408 B.C.	Euripides leaves Athens.
404 B.C.	Peloponnesian Wars end in

Sparta's victory over Athens. Oligarchy takes over in Athens, and ensuing terror.

399 B.C.   Death of Socrates.

384 B.C.   Birth of Aristotle.

380 B.C.   Death of comic playwright Aristophanes.

367 B.C.   Death of Dionysius I, ruler of Syracuse in Sicily. He is succeeded by his son Dionysius II.

353 B.C.   King Mausolus dies in Asia Minor and is buried in the Mausoluem, which becomes one of the Seven Wonders of the ancient world.

Recommended Reading

Scott Buchanan, ed., *The Portable Plato* (Viking Penguin, 1977)

Richard M. Hare, *Plato* (Oxford University Press, 1983)

Richard Kraut, ed., *The Cambridge Companion to Plato* (Cambridge University Press, 1992)

Plato, *The Trial and Death of Socrates: Four Dialogues* (Dover, 1992)

Karl Popper, *The Open Society and Its Enemies*, vol. 1: *The Spell of Plato*, 5th rev. ed. (Princeton University Press, 1966)

Index

Academy, 33–34, 40, 49, 51
Aegina, 15, 31–32
Aristotle, 9, 18, 51
Augustine, Saint, 28, 53

Christianity, 26, 46, 49, 52
Codrus, 15

Delphic Oracle, 21
Democritus, 12
Dialectic, 16
Diogenes Laertius, 36, 63
Dion, 29, 40–44
Dionysius the Tyrant, 29–32
Dionysius the Younger, 41–44

Grove of Academe, 32–33, 40

Hecademus, 33–34
Heidegger, Martin, 7
Heraclitus, 12

Justinian, 49

Kant, Immanuel, 28

Mandeville, Bernard de, 29

Neoplatonism, 52–53
Nietzsche, Friedrich Wilhelm, 7

Platonism, 51–53
Plotinus, 52
Popper, Karl, 65
Pre-Socratics, 7–13, 16–17
Pythagoras and the Pythagoreans, 8–12, 22, 27

Russell, Bertrand, 10

Socrates, 7, 16–19, 35, 40, 47, 61, 62
Solon, 15

Thirty Tyrants, 18

Thoreau, Henry David, 27

Wittgenstein, Ludwig, 13, 21, 22
Works: *The Apology,* 20–21; *Crito,* 20; *Euthyphron,* 20; Image of the Cave, 24; *The Laws,* 63–64; *Phaedo,* 20, 60–62; *The Republic,* 35–46, 57–59; *The Symposium,* 47; *Theaetetus,* 60; Theory of Ideas (or Forms), 48–49; Theory of Time, 26–28

Xenophanes, 12

A NOTE ON THE AUTHOR

Paul Strathern has lectured in philosophy and mathematics and now lives and writes in London. A Somerset Maugham prize winner, he is also the author of books on history and travel as well as five novels. His articles have appeared in a great many publications, including the *Observer* (London) and the *Irish Times*. His own degree in philosophy was earned at Trinity College, Dublin.